Wife. Mom. Entrepreneur.

23 Tips and Lessons to Juggling It All

Lanise Herman-Thomas
Janine Smalls-Gueye

Wife. Mom. Entrepreneur. 23 Tips & Lessons to Juggling It All

Copyright © 2016 Lanise Herman-Thomas & Janine Smalls-Gueye

All rights reserved. No part of this book may be reproduced or transmitted in any form or by any means without written permission of the author.

ISBN: 978-0-9837182-6-0

Library of Congress Cataloging-in-Publication: 2016946331

Perfectly Imperfect Publishing Company, LLC
Decatur, Georgia

Printed in the United States of America

Acknowledgements

First of all, we would like to thank our connect, God, which art in heaven, through you all things are possible.

To our loving husbands, who have supported our every decision—even when it seemed crazy and took all of your money (LOL). We thank you.

To our children, thank you all for being patient, supportive, and understanding.

To our parents, who helped mold us in to the women we have become today, we thank you for your motivation, support, and investments.

Love,
Lanise & Janine
The Tutors

Introduction

The Scrambled Brain

I need to do the laundry, prepare the kids' lunch and snack for school, and make dinner for the family. I have to meet a very important deadline so I can seal the deal. I still have not prepared for tomorrow's conference meeting. Oh God! It's my night to give the hubby a massage.

Have you ever heard the saying, "I have too many tabs open in my brain?" It's when you're thinking of too many things at one time and finding it hard to successfully get things done. This dilemma happens often as a *Wife. Mom. Entrepreneur.* Although the titles *Wife. Mom. Entrepreneur.* may appear very different, in all actuality they are very much alike. The roles and tasks of a *Wife. Mom. Entrepreneur.* all require an equal amount of attention, hard work, and dedication. My sister Janine and I know firsthand what it takes and how overwhelming it can be to juggle life as a

Wife. Mom. Entrepreneur.

Wife. Mom. Entrepreneur., while trying not to forget about yourself. Running a not-for-profit organization and two e-commerce boutiques, to investing in real estate, coaching and speaking at events—while needing to be loving, attentive wives and moms—was not always easy for us.

We had to figure things out and develop a solution to the problems and challenges we faced as we grew in our marriages, in motherhood, and in our businesses. We created a system that has helped us to successfully juggle our roles as *Wife. Mom. Entrepreneur.* We found that proper planning and not exceeding limits has been the essential key to our juggling act. Being a wife and mom while pursuing your dreams will take being an entrepreneur to another level. This role is not for the weak and overly emotional. Nothing is easy in entrepreneurship when you're sharing the role of wife and mom.

Entrepreneurship is rewarding, however, entrepreneurship does have a flip side. It can sometimes be very straining, stressful, and mind-boggling while trying to juggle all three roles. Just know that there is no such thing as a "perfectly balanced life." You just have to get as close to perfectly balanced as possible. You may see other entrepreneurs on your social media timelines who give off the impression that things are easy to obtain and accomplish, but please know that is not reality. Realistically, entrepreneurs put in a lot of hard work and groundwork. What you see on Facebook, Instagram, and other social media outlets are usually the fruits of their labor.

After reading this book, you will certainly be able to see the fruits of your labor too.

Introduction

It's hard work! Yes, but who is more qualified for the job than you? Join this phenomenon of women building legacies and making a name for themselves in the business world. There is no better time than now because women are out there crushing businesses, breaking barriers and stereotypes like never before—all while packing the kids lunch, attending parent-teacher conferences, and keeping their husbands happy (😜).

It's your time! So, get off of social media admiring the other girl bosses and beef up the GIRLBOSS that is in you. If you have not already began to balance your life as a *Wife. Mom. Entrepreneur.,* no worries. We wrote *Wife. Mom. Entrepreneur.* with 23 tips and lessons as a hands-on guide just for you and all the women like you, who are like us (wives, moms, and entrepreneurs) all-in-one. We have provided insightful and encouraging topics with a sneak peek at our real-life journeys and experiences as a *Wife. Mom. Entrepreneur.*

Wife. Mom. Entrepreneur. is an easy-read. We have written topics with specific interests allowing you to refer back to the area that speaks directly to you—even after you have read it from cover to cover. We want women to know that they are not alone as they struggle to sustain their sanity in figuring out how to be the best wife, loving and caring mom, and accomplished entrepreneur. In this book, we have provided you with the tips and exercises we used to make our road to success less stressful while building our businesses and maintaining our family life. This book will serve as your lifelong reference book. It will be the only *Wife. Mom. Entrepreneur.* guide you will need while building your business.

Table of Topics

The Cheating Wife. 1
The Decision 7
The Vision 11
I Did It On Purpose 17
Bad Parent 23
Happiness is a Decision. 33
I Need Help. 49
The Life Support 53
Be Organized 63
False Evidence Appearing Real 69
Goals. 73
Distractions. Distractions. Distractions. 79
Human Resource 87
Pay It Forward 93
It's Out of Your Hands 97
Collaborate/Partner. 101
Celebrating Small and Large Achievements. 107
God Bless My Naysayers 111
Be Encouraged 115
Closing Notes 117

> "No matter how busy you are, you must take time to make the other person feel important."
>
> — MARY KAY ASH

The Cheating Wife

(Lanise's Story)

My husband and I were the best of friends. We met in 2006 and had an unbreakable bond. We enjoyed each other's company. He was and still is a natural comedian; he keeps me laughing. During our time of dating, he constantly complained about hating his job. I encouraged him to pursue his passion of being an entrepreneur full-time. In 2009, we decided to make our relationship last forever. We completed a series of marriage counseling, then made it official. We got married. That was one of the happiest days of my life. About two years into our marriage, I decided I no longer wanted to be employed by someone else. I had grown a desire to work for myself and create a legacy of wealth for my family.

I partnered with my sister Janine and two of our friends, and we began a magazine company named *Rep Your Borough* magazine. That company was the birth of my adult

Wife. Mom. Entrepreneur.

entrepreneurial life and as expected in any infancy stage, it required care, nurturing, and attention—pretty much what a mom would give to her child or what a wife would give to her husband. I devoted pretty much all of my time to business. Business had become the most important thing to me. I lived, breathed, and ate our business literally every day, all day and a lot of the time into the wee hours of the night.

What did this do to my personal life—my duties as a wife and mother? It caused unfaithfulness, disappointments, mistrust, and broken hearts. I began making broken promises to my children, planning family outings, indoor events and not keeping my word. I cheated on my husband and children with my business. Yes, this happened. I felt that this business meant so much that I completely abandoned my family. My husband was neglected the most. I had too many tabs open—a scattered brain with no order. At that time, I had no clue on how to juggle being a *Wife. Mom. Entrepreneur.* I gave too much of myself to entrepreneurship and in return, my husband "Monica Lewinsky'd" me. That's the harsh truth. If ever there were a reason to take a step back and close some tabs, that was it!

Unfortunately, I had to find out how important it is to organize, prioritize, and close some open tabs the hard way. I had forgotten about the importance of game night with the kids and family, date night with hubby (including the late night conversations we used to have), and most importantly, general family time and keeping promises.

I can't lie. What he did blew my mind! He went out and had another woman to give him oral sex. Ladies, we know how we are about our men, especially when you know you have a good one. It made it hard for me to function. At times, I felt like I couldn't go on. Things had definitely changed and my marriage as I knew it would never be the same—not only because of his infidelity, but because of *our* infidelity. I had cheated, too. I was as much to blame as he. Although I had not physically engaged with an individual, just as worse, I had become emotionally and physically involved with something else. I put my business before my husband, leaving him vulnerable, and allowing our marriage to be targeted.

While going through the motions, I began to question myself. Did I make the wrong decision to become an entrepreneur? Should I have continued working a set 9 to 5 making someone else richer? This made me think of Langston Hughes. Should I have given up on my dreams? What happens to a dream deferred? I wasn't trying to find out. I needed my husband. He was my supporter. He supported my dreams, not only by motivating me, but he financially supported my goals and I had the nerve to cheat on him first with my business. I knew I had to fix things, but we had to fix things and take accountability for the damage we had done.

Eventually we dissolved the company due to the lack of commitment of all parties involved. This business venture taught Janine and I when doing business or partnering, it is imperative that all involved must be on one accord to successfully flourish. In July 2007 we incorporated our nonprofit. But it wasn't until 2012 that we became serious entrepreneurs. Although we had a business before, this time it was different.

Wife. Mom. Entrepreneur.

Today my husband and I stand stronger than ever. He is my everything. I'm blessed to have a husband who supports my aspirations and business. I hope after sharing my start-up story, you use that information as a what-not-to-do when starting out as a *Wife. Mom. Entrepreneur.*

> "In relationships, it's important to be able to identify your rights and your wrongs and own it."
>
> — LANISE HERMAN-THOMAS

> "I chose to be a working wife and mother. Why should I compromise on either?"
>
> CHANDA KOCHHAR

The Decision

Dreams of working with the youth and women was on repeat in our brains. Night dreams turned into daydreams. Our desire to leave our jobs had become persistent. Lanise and I would call each other and talk until the wee hours of the morning discussing our visions and plans for our not-for-profit organization. The dreams we were having began to consume our lives. They were so real, vivid, and in living color. We incorporated the organization in 2007 thinking, *Yes, we are in business.* However, business was at a stand still and did not operate because our families and full-time jobs interfered. There just was not enough time in a day. We realized that operating a fully functioning organization would take full-time work. Lanise finally made the decision to leave her job in 2010 and I shortly after in 2012.

It was not until we both made the decision to work full-time on our dreams and aspirations that we saw our

Wife. Mom. Entrepreneur.

organization flourish. Immediately we housed a facility that could hold the capacity of twenty-five hundred persons and was New York State licensed to service one hundred twenty-five youth. In July 2012, we began to operate business. From July to December we had only earned $6,093 and most of that money was not made until October 2012. We were determined that would not be the end of us. We got busy. We established partnerships, became marketing experts, and networked like never before. We went to our community boards and our local politicians offices.

Being a *Wife. Mom. Entrepreneur.* takes commitment, a different mindset, and a strong will to succeed. Success is not overnight and patience is definitely needed in business. If you're going to put in hard work for a company, let it be your own. Do it for yourself and your family. Be willing to shed blood, sweat, and tears for your dreams—the company you will build, and the legacy you want to leave behind for your children. We now have five revenue streams for our organization, not to mention our for-profit companies—all of which are in partnership with each other. We are immensely proud of the decision we made to leave our jobs and work on our entrepreneurial career. We are still dreaming. But the dreams are now bigger and better.

Write down your dreams on paper. If you have more than one dream that you aspire to attain, note it. Try to note your dreams in order of importance.

The Decision

What are your dreams?

> "Write the vision, and make it plain upon tables, that he may run that readeth it. For the vision is yet for an appointed time, but at the end it shall speak, and not lie."
>
> HABAKKUK 2:3 (KJV)

The Vision

We cannot tell you how important it is to have a vision and to write it down. Not just in becoming a boss, but in life period. I remember watching reality TV show *Runs House* for the first time. I heard Rev. Run, from the legendary hip-hop group Run-DMC, tell the story of how he got his first house in Queens, New York. I forgot which one of his kids he was talking to, but Rev. Run recalled the time when he wrote a little note to the homeowner saying that one day he would buy that house. And he did. The reason this stuck in my head is because it showed the power of writing down something and it coming to pass.

We can truly testify to writing the vision and making it plain. We sat down and made a vision board of all the things we wanted to accomplish, whether it was material items, educational goals, family goals—it didn't matter. We sat down at Janine's house and went through every magazine

Wife. Mom. Entrepreneur.

we owned, found images that represented what we wanted, and pasted them on our board. I kid you not. I had about twelve of the things I placed on my vision board to come to pass in less than a year. Now look at God! We encourage you to try this method and watch what happens.

The Vision

TIPS

Have a vision board party! It's simple, fun, and well worth it! Here is a basic list of things you'll need:
1. Magazines
2. Glue sticks
3. Scissors
4. Stickers (You can find some with quotes but this is optional)
5. Presentation board to paste your magazine clippings, and/or quotes that represent what you visualize for yourself.
6. Pen
7. Paper

With these basic things, you can create your own vision board. When you complete your board, post it in your house where you can see it everyday and start envisioning yourself obtaining these things. Start seeing yourself juggling life as a *Wife. Mom. Entrepreneur.*, having the happiest marriage, being the best mom you can be, and having a successful career as an entrepreneur doing what you love. Whatever it may be, you must get into action.

> "Write it down on real paper with a real pencil and watch sh-t get real."
>
> ERYKAH BADU

> "Sometimes you need to step outside, get some fresh air, and remind yourself of who you want to be."
>
> UNKNOWN

NOTES

I Did It On Purpose

Wake up every day anxious and ready to fulfill your life's desires. You are not a part of the walking dead—you know that show on television with the walking dead zombies who are just walking with no direction, dragging their feet? That's not *who* you are nor *what* you are. You are alive and breathing and a wonderfully fulfilled life awaits and welcomes you. It's time for you to tap into the living you. Yes! That person exists. The YOU (who you desire to be) is waiting for YOU to put to death the YOU who is keeping YOU from achieving your desired goals. We mean to literally create a mental death certificate for the confusion, uncertainties, fears of anything or for anyone—give it a mental funeral.

Just as we give mental funerals, we also have birthday celebrations for positive and significant life changes. It gives us a reason to celebrate one another and ourselves and to give life to the significant new achievements that give us greater purpose in life.

We recall a time when we just existed. We were not conscious of our appearance. We were just comfortable wearing jogging pants or leggings every day. We were unhealthy (both over 200 pounds) living paycheck to paycheck and borrowing from Peter to pay Paul. One day while I was out shopping, I ran into one of my nieces and she walked right pass me. She didn't even recognize me. I was happy she didn't recognize me because I looked horrible, and I didn't feel like lying about why I looked the way that I did. I had on a scarf with a hat, T-shirt, and some oversized jogging pants. You get the picture.

But I couldn't be upset with her for not recognizing me because I didn't even recognize myself. The saddest part of that day is that I was trying to convince myself by justifiably saying, "Please! It's okay. I have four kids, a husband, and I work hard. I don't have time to be getting dressed trying to look cute for people." That was the wrong self-guidance. It's not about just looking cute for people but ultimately yourself. When you look good, you feel good. And when you feel good, you perform great!

The truth of the matter was that we were not living a fulfilled life. We were not doing what we were designed to do. Our desires were not being met. We had our beautiful children and our wonderful husbands, but we were working for others. We had no ownership and control over our careers. At that time, we had good life intentions, but were living in contrast to our greatness—very passively and settled. We were both mentally challenged and mentally unhealthy. We knew we had hit a low. We had to become bounty hunters and take back our lives. Bounty hunters are hired to protect and recover a bail agent's investments. We figured out our worth. Our mental health was our greatest asset. It was going to be the tool to help us make our best investments, so we had to protect it.

We recovered ourselves and hit the gym. We ate healthy, threw away all of our old clothes, and purchased new ones. We changed our way of thinking and doing things, and "threw up the deuces" to our jobs. We prayed night and day and surrounded ourselves with inspiring and like-mined people.

Ladies, we should always leave the house ready to be impressionable. Lead with a purpose. Be mentally sharp, physically healthy, and confident. Always be in control of your life and fulfill your life's purpose *with* purpose. Think about the one thing that you do best and enjoy doing. It's the thing that you do better than anyone else, and it makes you feel happy and fulfilled. What do the people around you say you do best or constantly compliment you on?

Once you have figured out your gift, skill, or talent (maybe all three), it will set you aside from the rest. It was given to you on purpose. Use it for your purpose and do it on purpose. Go at your own pace. Do something every day that makes you feel good, gets you excited, and brings you closer to attaining your life's goals and aspirations.

Wife. Mom. Entrepreneur.

Insert your answers and use this table to identify your purpose.

What are my gifts, talents, and skills?	What do I enjoy doing? What am I absolutely good at doing?	What do people say I am good at doing?

This chart is available for FREE download at www.wifemomentrepreneur.com

> "When you find your purpose, you have positively elevated above conscious expectations (P.E.A.C.E)."
>
> JANINE T. SMALLS-GUEYE

> "A happy mother is a good mother; and if work makes you hum, your whole family sings along."
>
> UNKNOWN

Bad Parent

The feeling of guilt can consume you. Have you ever questioned your parenting decisions? Am I being a bad parent because I'm working? Am I neglecting my child? The answer is no. We are parents of children ranging from ages twenty-three all the way down to a one-year-old. Being a mom is one of the most amazing gifts from God. It is a job that God trusts you to do your best. When you decide to work, whether it is inside the home or outside the home, it's a big deal.

You may begin to feel guilt. Sometimes the decision to work isn't yours. It may be more of a need as opposed to a want. Most moms begin to feel guilty and begin to ask questions like, "Why am I not at home taking care of my kids?" or thinking *I'm a bad mom because I can't afford to stay home with my kids.* Does this sound like you? Well, you have company because we felt the same way too.

Wife. Mom. Entrepreneur.

Let's keep it real. If you're working for someone else or if you're working for yourself, what difference does it really make? You cannot live for your children. You must live for yourself. I always refer to the instructions the flight attendants give on a plane. In case of an emergency, they always instruct you to place the breathing mask on yourself before helping your child. Why is this you say? Well, if you're not okay, then how can you help your child? Apply the face mask to the child first and you will die. Then what? What good are you to your child? I always apply this lesson to my life. If I'm not happy, then how can I be a good, effective parent?

By working for yourself, it allows you to make time to attend class trips, bake cookies with the kids, and be an active parent. I find myself more active in my children's lives now more than I did when I was working a regular 9 to 5. I'm able to attend recitals, parent meetings, and even volunteer at their schools when I want. Most weekdays, my kids get to see me at 3 p.m. as opposed to 7:30 p.m when I was working for someone else. So, if you do find yourself battling with the question of whether or not you're a bad parent, allow us to answer it for you. No, you are not a bad parent and your child is not being neglected. Be accepting of the fact that having to work—whether it's for yourself or for another company—is something that normally has to be done to sustain life.

Guilt can literally consume you. It has the ability to take over your mind and make you completely dysfunctional. You may even ask yourself, "Is there something wrong with me?" "Why don't I want to stay with my kids?" On many occasions, we've literally cried about this—especially in the

Bad Parent

beginning because when you're developing and branding your company, a lot of your time is given to your business. You will miss out on some of your kids' events and you will not always be available for game night, a night out to eat, or to watch a movie.

To help us get over the guilt of being consumed by entrepreneurship, we developed our "pep talk" with words of reinforcement and encouragement. Our pep talks help remind us of the reasons we decided to follow our dream of becoming entrepreneurs. We would ask simple but powerful questions that would quickly get us back on track from Guilt Boulevard. Although we have each other, the questions we ask ourselves during our pep talk can be asked individually. Here are three of our power questions:

Why did I choose entrepreneurship?

_____
_____
_____
_____
_____
_____
_____
_____

Wife. Mom. Entrepreneur.

How will my children and family benefit from me being my own boss instead of working for someone else?

_____
_____
_____
_____
_____
_____
_____
_____
_____

What type of legacy do I want to leave for my children?

_____
_____
_____
_____
_____
_____
_____
_____
_____

Bad Parent

Oh, lawd! Don't take me on a guilt trip!

The guilt from others can come from strangers and even worse, your own friends and family.
"What if it doesn't work?"
"Don't you think it would be better to have a real job?"
"Hmm! You're crazy. You're not thinking straight." Or how about this one:
"You're wasting time trying to build a business when you can be working at a regular job and still be with your kids."

It sometimes seems as if people literally go out of their way to apply added guilt to your already full plate of guilt. You have to sometimes laugh at these "judgy" people. You know the people we're talking about. The ones who act as if they get paid to wear a black gown and bang a gavel judging your mere existence. Many of these "self-appointed judges" have never stepped out on faith nor have they ever did anything other than what society says is the right way of life.

You should never allow anyone to throw guilt on you for your decisions to be your own boss. You must know that the decision you made to follow your dream to be a entrepreneur is the right decision for you and your family. Do not care what anyone else thinks about what you do—ever. You may encounter people who may or may not be aware of the judgmental tone they use when they hear you say that you're a *Wife. Mom. Entrepreneur.*. They ask critical questions like, "Who's raising your children if you're an entrepreneur?" or "How involved can you be in your child's day-to-day life if you are an entrepreneur?"

Wife. Mom. Entrepreneur.

I have an awesome story to share about a judgy individual. Not long after I gave birth to my youngest daughter, I traveled to London for training. My youngest was five months old and had to travel with me because I was weaning her from breastfeeding. I paid all of my youngest sister's expenses to travel to London to babysit while I was in training. While I was there, one of my colleagues had the audacity to say, "You shouldn't have young children while working. You should be at home raising your kids first." I said to myself, "Wait, what? What planet did she come from?" My initial reaction was to bite off her head saying, "Mind your business. Don't worry about my life!" Instead, I actually responded politely. "I cannot imagine not working because I am a mom. I am more than capable of doing both. Thank you."

"Mom, I wish you didn't work."

In the case of The Children versus The Moms: The Moms, you have been found guilty!

There's something about the way my youngest daughter JalaSky and my nephew Chasey would ask, "Mom, why do you have to work?" that would fill your eyes with tears. "I wish you didn't work." That guilty feeling of *Maybe I am working too much and not spending enough time with the children* tries to set in. Janine and I learned to deal with the guilt that we felt from our kids' questions by explaining that we're working to leave behind a legacy for them and their siblings. We let them know that we are our own bosses, and work so that they won't need to work as hard as we did. It's refreshing as well as rewarding to be able to talk to your children about what you're doing and how it benefits them.

Wife. Mom. Entrepreneur.

Guilt Be Gone List

- ✓ As much as you can, involve your children in the work that you're doing. For example, A. Take the kids to events or bring them onsite if and when it's safe. B. Have them to assist in little ways (e.g. Chasey helps by sweeping the classrooms and handing out flyers.).
- ✓ Talk to your kids as much as you can about what you do.
- ✓ Set aside time to do things with your kids. This should be much easier since you are the one who's setting your work schedule.
- ✓ Create special, memorable traditions with your kids. For example, every month, you can watch your kid's favorite movie or create a new dance, handshake, flavor of ice cream, etc.
- ✓ Carve out time to play games, attend your kid's trips, recitals, etc. Be sure to get their calendar and build your work week around their scheduled events.

Bad Parent

- ✓ Pop up after school once in a while.
- ✓ Go for a bite to eat and talk.
- ✓ Truly devote your time to your children. Be present when you're present. Turn off your phone and stay away from your computer.
- ✓ Always, always let them know how much you love them!

If you decide to work as an entrepreneur, you may feel guilty. If you don't work, you may still feel some kind of guilt either way you slice it. Don't spend too much time dwelling on it. You'll just create more issues than solutions. So, in the words of Dory from Disney's *Finding Nemo,* "Just keep swimming. Just keep swimming."

Always Remember:
- ✓ I am a great mom.
- ✓ I am building an empire.
- ✓ My kids will be proud.
- ✓ I am proud of myself.
- ✓ I set the tone and make the rules.
- ✓ I am in control of my destiny.

> "It's important to make someone happy and it's important to start with yourself."
>
> UNKNOWN

Happiness is a Decision

There is nothing more important than personal happiness. There was a time when Lanise and I had given so much of ourselves being a *Wife. Mom. Entrepreneur.* Everyone around us was happy. Business was blooming but at the end of the day, we lacked personal happiness. We were so consumed with giving our time to everything and everyone that we forgot how to involve ourselves in the little and big things that made us happy.

The Lifeguard

Ladies, we have to make the decision to be happy despite all external factors. You are your own lifeguard, so be ready to apply CPR to your happiness at all times. How do I apply CPR to my happiness you ask? You **C**ontrol, **P**rotect, and be ready to **R**esuscitate when needed. Your happiness is your responsibility. Live for yourself. You cannot and will not be able to please everyone. Be okay with saying the word *no* and get comfortable with it. Say it again, "No." Say "No" and mean no. Do not feel bad about using that awesome word. It's actually refreshing and reduces stress and unhappiness.

We have listed some of the ways you can create your own happiness.

Change Your Mind, Change Your Attitude

Your mindset is a tool! How you think can adversely affect your attitude. If you are sitting around, speaking and thinking negative things about yourself or finding a problem in everything and everyone else, don't expect to be happy. You have to find what is awesome about you. Start with your achievements, accomplishments, your set goals and met goals, and significant travels. View yourself as being great no matter what. Find the good in people and think about why that person or persons are in your life. What joy and purpose have they brought to your life?

If a person constantly brings the worse out of you or brings you grief and sadness, get rid of them ASAP. They have no right to be in your life. Your perspective, perception, and focus have to be positive. What matters most is what's fit for your life's happiness.

1. Happy Wife (Janine's Story)
All Roads Leading to DIVORCE

I am going to be honest. Unlike Lanise, a few months after the "I Do's," I found myself incredibly unhappy. I had this grand 'ol misconception of what marriage was. Ladies, marriage is not just about the wedding and the honeymoon. It's a whole lot more. Marriage is ups and downs. It's explosive and mild. It's fun and filled with laughter. But it's also disappointments, tears, and dislikes. It's transparent, vulnerable, love, and compromise. But ultimately, your marriage should be a major part of your happiness forever!

However, the one thing it cannot be is divorce. That ugly word brings death to your union. At one point, I even thought that I wanted a divorce. I went as far as filing the papers and serving my husband. When I served him, it knocked the wind out of him. As he took a seat, with an addled look on his face, it was as if I had drugged him. He let out a soft yet aggressive whisper saying, "So, it's just that easy for you?" Seeing him in such a disoriented state, barely able to speak, broke my heart and frightened me. I could not even respond. I knew that I had let him down.

Then all of a sudden with a strong voice he says, "I'm not signing this. I love and want my family."

Today I am so grateful that he is a man of God and divorce for our family is not in his vocabulary. See, at that time, I really thought that I was doing something. I had grown tired of minor arguments, not speaking, and holding grudges. He was ego-tripping and letting his pride lead him in his marriage and so was I. My ego was so huge that it ran me to the courthouse. I allowed so many negative thoughts to consume me. I was thinking, *Yeah, I'm going to serve him his walking papers and show this motherf-cker that I ain't playing with him.*

Serving him with those papers did change things. It helped me realize how immature I was being over trivial things. But for my hubby, it was the creation of fear and distrust. I had stolen my husband's confidence to be a husband. We had to rebuild and restore trust, learn how to love unconditionally, and accept each other for who we are. I had to stop thinking selfishly and thinking like a little girl with fairytale dreams of marriage and accept my real-life marriage for what it is.

NEVER, NEVER, NEVER SPEAK POORLY ABOUT YOUR HUSBAND TO FRIENDS AND FAMILY MEMBERS.

Too many women make the mistake of sharing last night's argument or bad mouthing their husbands to their families and friends.

When you have forgiven or forgotten, they have not. I have made this mistake not once or twice, but a few times. Instead of talking to my husband about how he or the argument made me feel, I, being overly emotional, went and shared my thoughts with friends and family.

Let me tell you. That was not smart at all because I had friends and family who turned into my personal security guards, therapists, and attorneys. Their advice and how they handled my personal information was not always good. They

Happiness is a Decision

were having side conversations about my marriage with others and when I had forgiven my spouse and moved on, they did not. When my husband and I worked it out and I was happy, some of the same people with whom I shared my frowns now found it hard to accept my smiles. Be careful of what you say about your marriage and your husband, and be careful with whom you share your intimacy.

He is not a mind reader!

The worst thing to think is that your husband already knows. A lot of the little arguments my husband and I had came from my expectations of him already knowing what I wanted of him. We would talk about a subject and I would leave the conversation believing he had understood. After a series of serious conversations, we pinpointed our problem. We realized that we were experiencing a bad case of cultural differences. My husband is from Senegal, West Africa where men are very dominate and make money for their families. The women are caretakers and are very domesticated. Coming in to our marriage, my husband was and still is a great provider. But cooking and cleaning and having to be hands-on with our babies was not his thing. I did not understand this at all. Prior to marriage, he lived on his own. His house was always clean, and he claimed that he knew how to take care of children.

I thought I had asked all the right questions prior to marriage, but after a few months and definitely after the birth of our daughter, I realized that we shared different meanings of pretty much everything. My husband's idea of taking care of the kids is providing food, clothes, and smiling with them from time to time. He did not know how to change a pamper or feed the baby with a bottle. In fact, he could sleep through all types of cries—low pitch, high pitch—it didn't matter. He was not waking up. Cleaning? Forget about it. He couldn't clean to save his life. He didn't even know how to use an iron. He expected me or should I say he *assumed* that I would be the one cooking, cleaning, taking care of the children, and still working a full-time job. He would say things like, "You can handle that. That's a woman's thing." Thank God for love, understanding, and compromise.

    We still have our cultural differences, but we have a better understanding now. Instead of arguing, we just agree to disagree. Do not ever assume that your husband should know what you're thinking or that he should already know what you want. Converse about what your wants and expectations are in marriage and just in general. Marriage is a partnership. Always let your husband know when you need him. He wants and actually needs you to *need* him.

    Communication is the key to happiness in marriage. Hold on to all the beautiful things that made you say, "I Do" and constantly think about all the things you love about being a wife.

Happiness is a Decision

CHECKLIST

Happy Wife

- ✓ Exercise with your husband. Keep it sexy for you and him. Make sure you touch your toes with a sexy arched back, but no injuries please—that won't look good.
- ✓ Cook meals together.
- ✓ Go on dates.
- ✓ Give and get attention from your hubby.
- ✓ Accept hubby's flaws and uniqueness.
- ✓ Build up his weaknesses. Use and compliment his strengths.
- ✓ Do not ever compare your husband to another man.
- ✓ Do not compare your marriage.
- ✓ Always forgive.
- ✓ Read books to each other.
- ✓ Send loving texts.
- ✓ Have a sit down conversation daily.
- ✓ Always speak from the heart.
- ✓ Be transparent and vulnerable when needed.
- ✓ Never hold a grudge.
- ✓ Be open, honest, and respectful.
- ✓ Support each other's dream.

Wife. Mom. Entrepreneur.

- Do not nag. Say what you need to say one time. Let him marinate on it and allow him to think about what you have said.
- Have phone sex—even if he is in the house with you.
- Role play (be Roxanne tonight).
- Ask him to dance and strip for you.
- Dance with your hubby often.
- Share massages.
- Try sex toys (if you're both comfortable).
- Kiss and hug daily.
- Have at least two passionate kisses a week.
- Laugh, laugh, and laugh at his corny jokes.
- Do not take things too seriously.
- Allow hubby to be upset without taking it personally. Acknowledge that he is upset and see if you can be of assistance or just be understanding. If not, it is okay. Give him his space.
- Be spontaneous.
- Smile as often as possible.
- Be open to try new and different things.
- Be comfortable with the word *no*.

2. Happy Mom

Being a mom is the most fulfilling yet toughest job on earth. I do not know a single mom who does not want the best for her children. But being a happy mom is about knowing your limits.

- DO NOT overwhelm yourself.
- DO NOT stress over things you cannot control. Learn and get to know your child. Life as a mom will be less irritating because you already know what to expect from your child.
- DO NOT compare your child to other children.
- DO NOT compete with other moms.
- DO NOT COMPARE or COMPETE—PERIOD! Be a parent.
- DO NOT try to be a friend. The friendship will come later in life. For those of you with young children, the most important thing is to guide them into positive thinking and teach them how to display positive and happy behavior. Make sure your children are behaving age-appropriately. Instill excellent manners, values, and morals.
- DO NOT feel guilty when you have to lay down the law.

Wife. Mom. Entrepreneur.

CHECKLIST

Happy Mom

- ✓ Ask for help when needed or hire help as needed.
- ✓ Do not feel guilty when you have "me time" (spa day, dinner with girlfriends or friends, personal walk, etc.).
- ✓ Have family night.
- ✓ Take trips with your children.
- ✓ Take walks.
- ✓ Have plenty of talks.
- ✓ Be interested in what excites them.
- ✓ Support your children's ideas.
- ✓ If you have more than one child, have separate one-on-one time.
- ✓ Give lots of hugs and kisses.
- ✓ Dance and laugh.
- ✓ Have game night.
- ✓ Participate in charity or community work.
- ✓ Read books and watch movies.
- ✓ Tell your children something they do not know about you; perhaps something fun, educational, or inspiring from your childhood.
- ✓ Be comfortable with saying no.

3. Happy Entrepreneur

Balance. Balance. Balance. Life as a *Wife. Mom. Entrepreneur.* is the most rewarding thing in life. Having a wonderful marriage and loving husband, beautiful children, and your own successful business is such a blessing. The mere thought of it brings us happiness. If we could put *Wife. Mom. Entrepreneur.* on the title line of our business cards, and it would be appropriate for business, we would. It's just that awesome of a feeling. But with being a *Wife. Mom. Entrepreneur.* comes challenges and a lot of compromise.

The most important thing is your family. You need to keep them happy in order to be successful. As entrepreneurs, especially new entrepreneurs, you can easily work a one hundred hour week just to see your goals and ideas come into fruition. But as *Wife. Mom. Entrepreneur.* we have to set limits. That's the great thing about being an entrepreneur. You create your own work schedule—how many hours you work a day, how many days you work in a week, and where your work location will be for the day.

Wife. Mom. Entrepreneur.

CHECKLIST

Happy Entrepreneur

- ✓ Put your family first. Happy family = successful business.
- ✓ Accept failures; it's a part of business. Don't dwell on your failures. Dust yourself off and get back up. Failing leads to success.
- ✓ Be comfortable with saying no, especially in business. If it doesn't feel right or if it's not what you want, do not accept it.
- ✓ Create work hours that work for you as a wife and mom. You can always adjust as needed. Remember, you're the boss.
- ✓ Don't become overwhelmed. Take breaks.
- ✓ Work in the environment that best suits you.
- ✓ Network and build new partnerships.
- ✓ Stay within the trends for your market.
- ✓ Attend trainings and workshops in your line of business.
- ✓ Have fun doing what you love.

Happiness is a Decision

Happiness is very different for everyone. Make sure you are doing what makes you happy. I prefer to work from our office. Lanise prefers to work from home. That makes her happy. We make sure that we are happy daily. Even when failure or disappointment is present, we put on a smile. We know that smiling sends a signal to the brain that everything is or will be okay. Exercising and eating good food (in moderation) makes me happy. Shopping and catching great sales makes Lanise happy. Reading a good book and doing something for the less fortunate makes us both happy. And when we work with the youth of our not-for-profit, we feel fulfilled.

> "Housekeeping ain't no joke."
>
> LOUISA MAY ALCOTT

Janine Smalls-Gueye (from left), Sheila Lirio Marcelo, Founder, Chairwoman and CEO of Care.com, Lanise Herman-Thomas

> "Okay! The bills are washed, the laundry is paid, clothes are in the oven and the last load of dinner is in the dryer. It looks like I got my "To-Do" list finished!"
>
> UNKNOWN

I Need Help

If you plan to be a do-it-all, expect your completed duties to look just like this "To-Do" list. Don't be afraid to hire help. Yes, we said, "Hire help." This is something we learned the hard way. Some may think you're being "bougie" or lazy, but the fact of the matter is that we all need help. As a *Wife. Mom. Entrepreneur.*, you can spread yourself thin trying to accomplish everything you have on your list for the day. This is where an extra pair of hands can come in. Too expensive you say? Well, what if I told you that you could get a housekeeper for as little as ten dollars per hour on *www.care.com*? It's true. We have our housekeeper come to the house once or twice a week for four hours. This frees up tons of time and who doesn't like to come home to a clean house?

Now you can complete other duties such as helping with homework, answering emails, business planning, cooking, and preparing for the next day. We've found it to be very stress relieving. Hiring help will alleviate some of your stress and it is a great way to relax sooner than later. Now, we're not telling you that you MUST hire help. We're just telling you what worked for us and how hiring help has made things much easier for us to juggle other duties.

You may be thinking, *I can't afford it!* Oh, yes you can! By making small sacrifices, you can surely afford hiring a housekeeper at least once a week for a couple of hours—whatever your preference is. We made small sacrifices, and so can you.

Here are some ways you can make hiring a housekeeper affordable:

1. **Girls Night.** Instead of having a girls' night out (spending money on cabs, food, and drinks, which may cost anywhere between $50-$100), try purchasing a bottle of wine or your favorite drink, and drink at home alone or invite the ladies to come over. Here are a few of our favorite bottles: Sweet Bitch Wines ($10); Myx Fusion Moscato (4-pack $8-12); Bartenura Moscato ($12).

2. **Don't eat out as much.** This one was tough to give up. We are true foodies. We love Italian, African, Soul Food, Caribbean, and French cuisine. We could go on, but we will stop there. Cut back on eating out and prepare meals at home. You can save tons of money.

3. **Limit your spending on clothing.** We love bargain shopping, but we have to find other options sometimes. When you're at the retail stores, brace yourself and ask, "Do I really *need* to purchase another black blouse? Can I wear one of the twenty other black tops that I already have?" Avoid the mall and your favorite clothing store, and if you feel you really need to shop, check the thrift store in the more upscale neighborhoods.

4. **Coffee purchases.** Yes! We relaxed on the Starbucks purchases. Just think, a tall caramel macchiato costs $5. Now if you just make a cup a coffee at home for five days, you just saved $25. You can now afford two hours of housekeeping.

> "Unity is strength…when there is teamwork and collaboration, wonderful things can be achieved."
>
> MATTIE J.T. STEPANEK

The Life Support

Supportive Spouse

One of the most important people on your team is your mate—whether he is actually a part of the business or not. Our husbands are true gifts! Their support is like none other. Over the years, through all the ups and downs, failures and triumphs, they have been our constant support. Following your dream and building an empire takes dedication. It can be, and I stress, very overwhelming at times which can take a toll on you emotionally, physically, and mentally. You need or should I say MUST have a supportive mate who will be able to deal with what you will go through as an entrepreneur.

The lines of communication must be open at all times. This way he is abreast of what's going on with you and vice versa. There may be times when your spouse has to attend all the children's school meetings that you agreed to attend. He may have to sit-in at your son's soccer practice or your daughter's dance practice because something suddenly came

Wife. Mom. Entrepreneur.

up and now you can't make it. Or simply because you're completely burned-out and in desperate need of some good restful sleep. Yes! Sometimes I need ten full hours of sleep. A great and supportive spouse, who can see and understand your needs, makes all the difference.

Raising children is difficult in itself. Much less having to make doctors appointments, shopping for clothes, making sure the children are groomed and clean, homework, etc. Having to keep up with these things can be stressful and overwhelming. Now add being an entrepreneur on top. This is where it is important to have a supportive spouse. Sharing the tasks and responsibilities of raising your children benefits the entire family. You keep your sanity, the hubby is in the loop of all that is going on, and the kids see that both parents are active and invested in their development and well-being.

Supportive Spouse continued ... Sharing Responsibilities

Stop with the SUPER WOMAN ACT

We are not fictional characters. This is real life and real things happen every day. We as women often play many roles and take on so much responsibility, just killing ourselves when we don't have to. It's like we love to be overwhelmed. Let's start sharing the responsibility with our spouse. Remember, marriage is a partnership. Husbands and wives should be fully committed. Sometimes it just takes us wives to lead the way by planning things out.

The Life Support

Create a list for each child including all the activities that they are in or have coming up. Go over this list with your spouse while creating a calendar of events. This way you can arrange who will do what and when. I'm going to share a chart that I started using. This is what my husband and I use to stay organized for all activities, meetings, etc. We also add it to our iPhone so neither of us can have excuses. We have two kids. We insert whatever needs to be done in the chart and divide and concur. We find it best to do this every two or four weeks as things change. You can edit this chart to best fit you. On the chart you will notice the column for a backup system (B.U.S.). We do not live in a perfect world and will sometimes need to call in reinforcements.

If you're thinking, *I can do it. I don't like to ask for help,* let us remind you that we cannot do it all. Sometimes you need help. It is great to have a backup system. Ladies, communication is key to your sanity, so communicate, communicate, and communicate! This cannot be stressed enough.

Always Remember:
1. Communicate.
2. Be direct and always make sure both of you understand your role.
3. Sh-t happens. Roll with the dice and adjust to whatever changes arise.
4. Plan, plan, and plan. You will see how having a game plan in place will get things done without the added stress.
5. Be a team player, not super woman.

Wife. Mom. Entrepreneur.

The Who, What, Where Chart

Activity	Mom	Dad	Backup System	Both of Us
School Pick up				
Clothing Shopping				
Grocery Shopping				
Bath Time				
House Chores				
Bills				
School Activity				
Weekend Activity				

The Life Support

In case of emergency, break glass Backup System (B.U.S.)

We live in New York City. Trains get stuck; they go out of service, and even "go express," skipping your stop and making you late to pick up your kids. This is when your backup system comes in handy. We stated this before, but I must say it again. We as women for some reason or another do not like to ask for help. My sister Janine is definitely one woman who struggled with allowing herself to ask or accept help with her children.

Ladies, get over it! It takes a village to raise a child. I know you've heard that old saying before and it is still relevant today. Support outside of the home is very much needed and having a backup system does not take anything away from you. It does not lessen your ability to be a good mom. This is just reality and you need to be prepared for it. Just imagine you're hours away from home and your husband is stuck in traffic. Wouldn't you want to have backup players to step in and pick up your kids, or would you rather chance it and have your child at school wondering if their parents had forgotten about them?

Actually, this happened to me. One day, my then six-year-old daughter, JalaSky stood with her bus attendant in the front of our building because her dad was stuck in traffic on Franklin D. Roosevelt East River Drive. I was more than an hour away in a business meeting. It broke her dad's heart to see the tear stains on her face and to hear her say, "I thought you forgot about me." From that day forward, we created a backup system.

Wife. Mom. Entrepreneur.

Get A Backup System Before You Need It

Setting up the backup system can be an easy task depending on how many people and resources you already have on hand. First thing you should do:
1. List all of your friends and family who live in your area.
2. Find out what programs are available in your community (some provide pickup service).
3. Once you get your list together, be sure to communicate with the people who will be your backup players. Give the people on your list a call. Let them know that you've just enlisted them as your backup system.

This is your "in case of emergency, break glass" list. Now, if you need help drafting your players, here is a little script that you can use:

> *Hey, in case of an emergency where my husband or I can not get to the kids on time, I'd like to know if I can add you to my backup system list. I love that you love our kids and they enjoy being around you. You are one of my first choices when it comes to caring for our children.*

Now, exhale. It's over. You did it. You've conquered your fear of seeking assistance. People can only say yes or no. If they say yes, then add them to your list and move on to the next person. If the answer is no, then move on to the next person. It's that simple. Don't make a big deal out of the no's. I'm sure they will have good reasons for declining the opportunity. Once the calls are done and the list is made, email or text each participant who you've enlisted. This email or text should let them know how much you appreciate their help and to thank them for being a part of your backup system.

If you do not have friends or family members who can be a part of your backup system, speak to the school's Parent Association. Most of the parents in these associations are walking resources. They can help you locate after-school programs in the school or in the neighborhood.

Always Remember:
1. Have a backup system before you need it.
2. Have several backup players who are reliable. Take your time creating this list.
3. Have up-to-date phone numbers for all backup players. In the time of need, you must be able to speed dial your players.
4. Show your appreciation. It never hurts to send little tokens of appreciation whether it is a text, flowers and/or a fifty-cent Hallmark card, etc.
5. Both you and your spouse should be on the same page with the backup system and the players.
6. Ask other parents for recommendations regarding homecare providers and after-school programs.
7. Be sure to add your backup players to the pick up list at school. Don't be the parent with the backup who can't pick up!

Wife. Mom. Entrepreneur.

Supportive Team

The joys of a supportive team are like no other. A supportive team is very important in business and life in general. The people you will work with or choose to work with must be on one accord. We've learned that you cannot bring just anyone on your team. You will hear us say this a lot. Dismiss all negative people from the equation. Who specifically are we talking about you ask? Well, we're talking about friends, family, co-workers, employees, and anyone who is a member of your team.

If any of your team members are not giving you the support you need, it is imperative that you address the situation immediately. An example of a person being unsupportive can be as simple as the way that person talks to you. A person making jokes about your business ventures such as "When will you see the fruits of your labor? You've been working on that venture forever. Ha-ha, stop wasting your time." These are just a few things that can arise and need to be handled right away. We're not saying to cross that person out of your life completely. If you and the person can fix the issue, then do so. However, if it's an unsalvageable situation, you must do what's right for you, your company, and the legacy you are building. Declare, "All toxic relationships get behind me!"

Do not be afraid to remove unsupportive people. I remember a few years ago when we hired someone at our youth center as a lead counselor. They had all the credentials, references, and personality. I mean, they had everything—the entire package, or so it seemed. Needless to say, once hired, this person demonstrated the complete opposite of what our company represents. This person was not a team player and didn't display respect

The Life Support

for others. Yes, this person was nice to administration, but they did not meet our company's expectations, so this person had to go. You have to be able to let go of toxic people. One bad apple will ruin what you are working so hard to build.

Let's talk about the people who you think would be obvious supporters. You may have tons of childhood friends (even friends from college), and co-workers who you hang out with. You would think that they would be the first to support you, right? Don't bet your last dollar on it, and do not set yourself up for disappointment. This is not true for all, but it does happen. Don't get us wrong. We have friends and family who will support us if we decided we wanted to build a bridge made of plastic forks alongside the Brooklyn Bridge, (LOL). *But they really would.*

The faster you get over the disappointment of friends and family not supporting your venture the better for you. It's been said many times that women are emotional thinkers and for many of us, it's true. You may be thinking, *Come on, now. I know I can count on Jane and Joe. We grew up together.* Nope! Not always. Let's state some facts. Not everyone wants to see you succeed. This is reality and you have to be okay with this. The shift in friends is real, and it happens fast.

As your vision for your life and business changes, so will the people around you. Those friends who you used to hang out with will dwindle away the minute you reach out in support of your business. This is all a part of building a successful business. Besides, at this point you want nothing but good vibes around you. You want people who make healthy deposits in your business and life.

> "With organization comes empowerment."
>
> LYNDA PETERSON

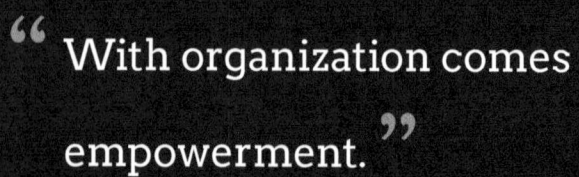

Be Organized

In the Scattered Brain introduction, we talked about having too many tabs open at once. This section of the book will guide you on how to properly plan and organize, so that you will be able to juggle multiple tasks without being overwhelmed. We can tell you from experience that it is very important to organize. This is one of the most important facts of being an entrepreneur. At one point in life, we thought we could remember everything. A list in your head will always have items not checked off. How can you raise babies, cook, clean, shop, spend quality time with the family, and remember to order your daughter's contacts? By the way, you still have to call maintenance for the leaky sink, pick up laundry, go to the drugstore because they have a sale on Albacore tuna, make a bank deposit, pay the babysitter, and oh, don't forget the 8:30 p.m conference call before your date with hubby in the bedroom.

Does this sound like you? This is something that happens much too often leaving you completely stressed out because at least five things on the *in-my-head-list* would be left off for the next day or pushed on to the next week. Not only were these items being left out, and the tasks were not getting done and/or being delayed, it isn't good for your health. I was in bed at night not getting enough sleep because I would think about all the things I accomplished or did not accomplish using the *in-my-head-list*.

One day while sitting in one of our board member's office, I was admiring how organized she was. "How are you so organized?" I questioned. I watched her go from list to list, in and out of binders with such ease. Not once did she have a puzzled look as to where she might have placed something. "I have a 'To-Do' list," she said. "It's what I stick to daily. I do not do anything without my 'To-Do' list." The board member gave me a few copies of her list and life became a lot better. This "To-Do" list is straight to the point and it works.

Get in the habit of listing the things you need to accomplish by highest priority first. For me, I use my "To-Do" list and copy it to my smart phone notes and reminders—which I have linked to my iPad. This method works for me because I don't always have my agenda book in hand. So, it's helpful to have my list in multiple areas. Again, this is what works for me. It may not be the way you do things, but for me I get the job done with this method. Lawd, the things you will accomplish with a list. Being able to check off things as they're being completed is something that deserves praise.

Check out this simple "To-Do" List:

"To-Do" List

Date	Task	Due Date	Done

Organizing, for some, comes easy. But for others, it doesn't. When you're young and kid-free, being disorganized isn't a big deal. Add *Wife. Mom. Entrepreneur.* to the mix and organizing becomes law. The lack of organizing can reduce your productivity, but when you organize your home and work life, it instantly saves you time. You avoid spending valuable time on hunting and searching for whatever is needed. You will gain more time *to do* what you like to do such as spending time with your family.

Wife. Mom. Entrepreneur.

Become Organized

1. Encourage everyone at home to put things where they belong. If everything is in its correct place, it will not be hard to find.
2. Plan ahead. If you prepare meals for the week ahead of time, there's no need to hustle finding meals at the last minute.
3. Use calendars. Your calendar should have everything scheduled for the week and month.
4. Be prepared. Take time each night to go over what's needed for the next day: The kids book bags are packed and by the door, clothes are laid out, lunch is packed and breakfast already planned to prepare. Oh, and ladies, don't forget to pack the pocketbook you plan on carrying. How many times have you left your identification (ID) in the pocketbook you wore the day before? Go over your list and check off things as they're completed.
5. Get some rest. Get to bed and shut your eyes. When a person is well rested, they can tackle their day more effectively.

Be Organized

6. Organize work projects with color tabs or labels. Using different colors for each subject can train your mind to easily identify each project by the color you assign it.
7. Organize work by its importance.

Always Remember:
- ✓ No one is perfect.
- ✓ Organizing reduces stress, so make stress reduction a priority.
- ✓ Organizing reduces clutter.
- ✓ Organizing saves time.
- ✓ Organizing will help you succeed in business.
- ✓ Being organized increases productivity.

> "If you push through that feeling of being scared, that feeling of taking risks, really amazing things can happen."
>
> — MARISSA MAYER

False
Evidence
Appearing
Real

OMG! What do we do now? Did we just jump out the window? How will we make ends meet in our households? What about rent? What about unexpected expenses? The fear was real! Fearing the unknown can hold you back from your dreams. You can never get to success with fear blocking what could be. We didn't have much money saved. We had to depend on our husbands to pull the majority of the weight in our homes. Thank God we have supportive spouses.

Fear is just that—it's fake. Although it may appear real, it's FALSE. We would be lying if we told you that getting over fear is easy. It is not. You will have those moments when you think about everything that can go wrong: *What if this happens or what if this doesn't work? How will I take care of my family? What if I fail?* And guess what? You already failed by not trying and staying restrained by your fears.

Do not get caught up in what you fear. You must identify your fears, no matter how many—address them and dismiss them. Many gifted individuals who aspire to become entrepreneurs give lifetime leases to fear. Whenever fear shows up with all its baggage say, "Fear, you cannot live here. You are evicted."

> "A strong woman looks a challenge dead in the eye and gives it a wink."
>
> — GINA CAREY

NOTES

Goals

Goal-setting is essential to every entrepreneur when it comes to seeing the results of what you set out to do. When you set measurable goals, you are sure to succeed. Ask yourself, "What is the goal and what do I need to reach this goal?" After you have figured out your goals, you need to develop a plan of action for reaching your goal. After much trial and error with unclear goals and wasted time, we created the A.T.M. method to guide us when developing our plan of action.

What is the A.T.M. method? It is how we take on any goal or idea that we pursue. The goal must be attainable, timed, and measurable. When you see the acronym A.T.M., which stands for automated teller machine, it automatically leads you to think of depositing and withdrawing money. Same concept applies here. Our A.T.M. method will certainly have you depositing and withdrawing success, new partnerships, and money.

(A) Attainable

Your goal should be attainable. Make sure the goal isn't vague and that it's straightforward. For example, "I want to have more partnerships." While this is a goal, it is very vague. Try including the amount of new partnerships you'd like to gain, the types of partnerships, and list various approaches to how you will set out to achieve your goal. How will you attain these partnerships? For example, "I will make three new partnerships within the first three months of this new year. My goal is to partner with A corp, B corp, and C corp." Setting detailed goals allow you to focus on your specific type of business.

(T) Time

Time is never to be wasted. We can never get back time. Once it's gone, it's gone. It is a must that you have a time limit. If you do not have time limits set, you run the risk of procrastinating. Time limits hold you accountable. Set a start date and a target date to have your goal completed. Be reasonable. Give yourself the time you will need to obtain the set goals. For example, the goal is to obtain three partnerships. You've identified all of the obstacles and needs in your goal as well as the questions that need to be answered.

Goals

Now allot the appropriate time needed for each partnership you're seeking. This includes researching the potential partners' company, listing the benefits of the partnership, etc.

(M) Measure

Is my progress measurable? Your goal should be measurable. You should be able to look at the progress you have made and measure the difference from where you started. For example, we started our business with no partnerships. Within the first year, we established ten new partnerships benefiting our organization.

Always Remember:

- ✓ A regular review of your goals is important. It will keep you on time and on track.
- ✓ Focus on "attainable" goals. Don't go bananas and create goals that will take you maybe five years to achieve. We don't want to discourage you at all, however, if you take things one year at a time, you will see progress that is measurable. Besides, you don't want to set yourself up for frustration. Save the five-year goal for your long-term goal. Focus on what you can accomplish within one year.
- ✓ Write down everything. The vision will become life, so keep your plans and goals on paper.

Wife. Mom. Entrepreneur.

A-
Can I reach this goal? Is it a challenge? Is it attainable?
T-
Do I have a time limit set? Start date? Target date?
M-
Is my progress measurable?

Sometimes you fall off track but don't worry too much. Give yourself a break. We are only human, and if you're like me, sometimes I want instant results. If you find yourself withdrawing no results from your A.T.M., give yourself a few days to regroup. Try changing your strategy to be less stressful and more realistic.

> "She was unstoppable not because she did not have failures or doubts. But because she continued on despite them."
>
> — UNKNOWN

> "Starve your distractions and feed your focus."
>
> UNKNOWN

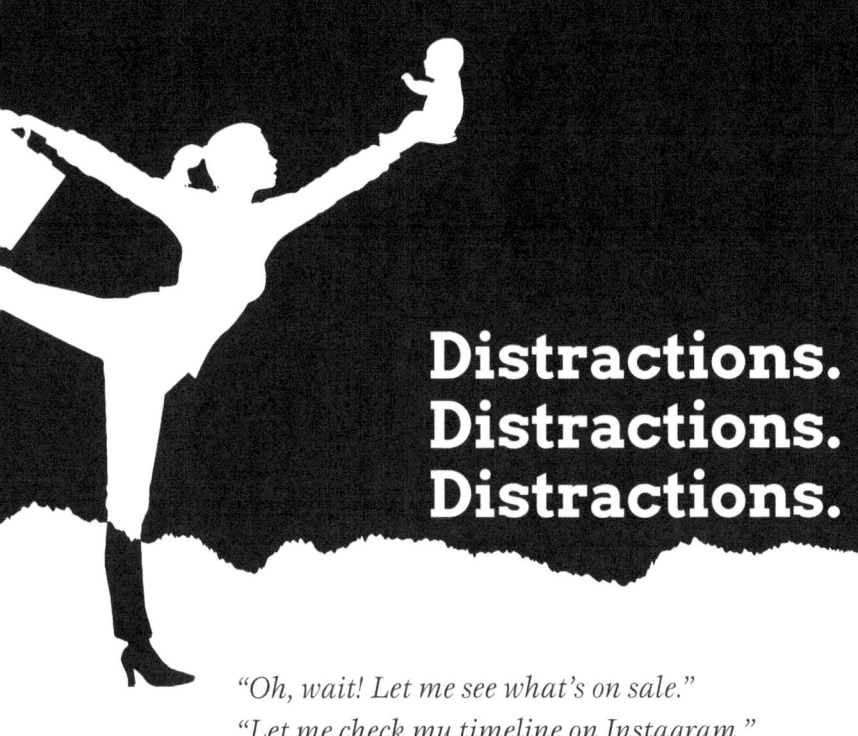

Distractions. Distractions. Distractions.

"Oh, wait! Let me see what's on sale."
"Let me check my timeline on Instagram."
"Hello! Where are you going girl?"
"Mom, can I have this?"

How many times a day does something distract you? We deal with distractions daily. If you add up all the distractions that you face, just imagine what you could've accomplished in that time. Yes, it's sad. We are easily distracted, so we had to pay attention to the time we were losing due to distractions. We used to love looking for sales and checking our Instagram timeline. Then we would call each other to discuss the sales or what we had seen on Instagram—not to mention small talk about our husbands and kids.

We've listed some of the top distractions we face and how we've reduced or eliminated them completely. Questions to think about:

1. What distractions do I face?
2. How will I deal with distractions?

Wife. Mom. Entrepreneur.

How to Eliminate Distractions

Phone Calls

Do not disturb. We may be thinking that button on our phone is not for us. We're a *Wife. Mom. Entrepreneur.* We have family, friends, and a business which means our phones cannot be turned off. Try setting special ringtones to all of your important contacts. If your phone rings while you're focused on your master plan, you will know if it's a need-to-answer call.

Social Media

Social media is a useful tool, however, it can also be a MAJOR DISTRACTION if not used properly. We all have people who we follow on social media for entertainment, inspiration, socializing, or just to keep up with our family and friends. First, it's reading about celebrities and their latest publicity stunt. Then we want to read all of the comments under their post and so on. Before we know it, we get pulled into a social media trance and we're stuck actually forgetting everything we were supposed to be doing. Set aside a time when you allow yourself to indulge in social media for your personal entertainment.

Distractions. Distractions. Distractions.

Emails

What does your inbox look like? I'm guessing you have tons of unread mail from your favorite magazines, blogs, online stores, potential business deals and junk mail, all NEEDING to be read and responded to. How can we complete any task if we're constantly checking our email the second we see a new notification? The solution? Scheduling email time. Setting a specific time to check emails will eliminate being consumed with reading and responding to mail all day.

The best time to schedule email time is during your lowest productivity time. For example, if your highest productivity time in the morning is reserved for getting the kids up, fed, and out the door, try to capitalize on your lowest productivity time after the kids are gone. Grab a cup of coffee, sit down, and click away.

Another way to eliminate emails as distractions, while working on your goals, is to turn your email notification OFF. Yes! Turn it off. If you cannot see the notification symbol, you are less tempted to open it. Once you reach your scheduled email time, you can turn it back on and get to reading and responding.

Wife. Mom. Entrepreneur.

The Internet

DO NOT OPEN! KEEP IT CLOSED! Step away from the browser.

The minute you click on the Internet browser, you're trapped. We become browsing zombies. Have you ever gone online looking for one thing, then a few minutes later found yourself searching another site looking for something else? I mean, what is it? Why do we get behind a computer and our mental "To-Do" list or shopping list instantly opens up? We begin searching and searching, forgetting all about what we should be doing.

The best way to not get sucked in and become a browsing zombie is to keep out. Say it with me, "If it's not work related, don't entertain it." Keep that browser closed. If you're not careful, this distraction can come at a big expense causing major setbacks, missed deadlines or goals that you've set for the day.

Distractions. Distractions. Distractions.

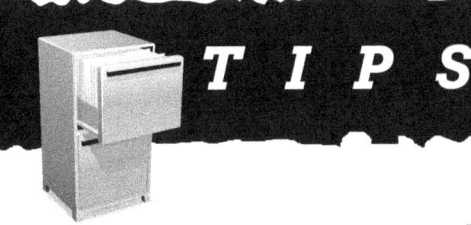

When You Get the Urge

- ✓ Give your brain some rest. We all need to take a mental break. Try taking advantage of the NO INTERNET time by just closing your eyes and taking in a few deep breaths.
- ✓ Sign out of all of your accounts during work time.
- ✓ Schedule Internet time after you've met your goals for the day. (There's nothing wrong with a little Internet browsing.)
- ✓ Utilize apps that can help you eliminate distractions.

People

Your husband, kids, family, and friends may be the biggest distractions of them all. People in general can be very needy causing you to fall off track, especially if you're the "go to" person.

- ✓ Try going into another room and placing a DO NOT DISTURB sign on the door.
- ✓ Go to the library. Before we had our offices, we did our work at our local library. Sometimes a different atmosphere such as the library can put you in a very productive mood and help you to really focus and get things done.
- ✓ Use headphones or ear plugs.
- ✓ Situate your home before you begin working. Make sure everyone has what they need before you sit down to work. Have your husband or backup player take the baton. Let them be the "go to" person during your work hours.

Distractions. Distractions. Distractions.

Always Remember:

1. Distractions can increase stress as well as halt your productivity.
2. Find the best method that works for you to eliminate stress.
3. Schedule EVERYTHING! If you stick to a schedule, there will be no time for distractions. Try setting an alarm or timer for every task on your list for the day. This will keep you on track and help you beat the clock.
4. Do not be distracted by things that have nothing to do with your goals.
5. Consistently do what works to keep you focused and undistracted.

> "Surround yourself with only people who are going to lift you higher."
>
> OPRAH

Human Resource

Surround Yourself with Likeminded People

Let me sigh! When we made up our minds to pursue life to its greatest potential, our everyday people began to disappear one after another. Certain conversations with our friends and families became unattractive because our once shared interest had disappeared. Then the calls stopped. But when that happens, just know that it was meant to be. It's normal and it happens. But sometimes with great gains, there will be some losses.

When you are aspiring to be great, you have to be selfish and choosy. You might even lose important and meaningful people in your life, like your childhood friends, family, and so called "best friends." We did—although now we know that they weren't so "best" anyway. It's not that we set out for things to go that way, but sometimes envy, jealousy, and common interests get lost. You don't have the same time that you once had. Know that you are the co-founder of your life. God gave you life—a brain that thinks and a heart and gut that feels. The infrastructure is up to you.

If your current "co's" cannot go half on gas to get you to the next destination, meaning if they cannot help you elevate to the next level, then it is time to recruit and execute. If you are wondering who or what your "co's" are, they are the prefix folks in your life—the co-worker, co-friend, co-lover, etc.

You have to think like the human resource department of a company. They only want the best to help the company grow and develop. You have to search for human capital and put yourself in places with people who think like you, want the same things as you (or more), and who are already in the area of business that you are pursuing. Seek people on social media who share your interests and introduce yourself. People can and will gladly assist you in being the best you.

Do not be afraid of the new you—the person who wants more, who's unapologetically confident (but not rude or cocky), and who knows where they're going but does not know exactly how to get there.

NETWORK. NETWORK. NETWORK. Think of yourself as a brand. You have to protect yourself. Be careful of who you are around and how you conduct yourself. Be mindful of who may be watching you. In business, people are at a place of growth and prosperity and they like that place. They like how it feels. They become protective and careful of who or what they allow into their social circle or even with whom they will do business. They will not want to partner or associate with you if you may possibly taint their image or brand. Stay away from negative, infectious people.

Remember, you are doing things differently this time. Be selective of who you associate with and who or what you have representing your brand.

On the following page is a strengths, weakness, opportunities, and threats analysis chart (SWOT). Once you have added the information, this will help you to analyze who should and should not surround you.

List the following:

1. **S**trengths that you and the people around you should posses;
2. **W**eaknesses that you should stay clear of that can damage you as you grow;
3. **O**pportunities that you and the people around you should present;
4. **T**hreats that you should avoid as an entrepreneur.

Wife. Mom. Entrepreneur.

Put Your Name Here:

Strength	Weakness	Opportunity	Threat

" You are not better than anyone, but you are better than anything. "

JANINE T. SMALLS-GUEYE

NOTES

Pay It Forward

Pay it forward! Do you hear the action in that expression? Paying it forward is an alternative act of giving. Let us be the first to tell you how great it makes you feel when you are gift giving. For us, we do it daily. We have a not-for-profit that we solely funded for many years, but as it grew, other people and companies began to pay it forward. We also find ways to be charitable.

For instance, one Christmas, we participated in the YMCA's Angel Christmas List where kids placed on the tree what they wanted for Christmas in the form of an ornament. We purchased things like cribs and mattresses to things as simple as sleepers. As a *Wife. Mom. Entrepreneur.*, being charitable brings true joy and happiness to our heart. Please know that our good works are not always in the form of monetary donations or purchases. Sometimes we will feed people at a soup kitchen and participate in toy

Wife. Mom. Entrepreneur.

and clothes drives. You can join a volunteer association or a community or local not-for-profit board. Join Habitat for Humanity (if your schedule permits) or help around the church and local schools.

Most importantly, as the Bible says, be a cheerful giver (2 Corinthians 9:7 NKJV). Commit to pay your tithes and offerings at church, mosque, synagogue, or wherever you call your place of worship. In the end, being able to give to someone who is less fortunate or to someone who may be in a temporary crisis makes your life as a *Wife. Mom. Entrepreneur.* so worthy!

> "Some people create their own storms & then get mad when it rains."
>
> — UNKNOWN

NOTES

It's Out of Your Hands

Let go of things you cannot change

In entrepreneurship, you have no time to "sleep" on opportunities. This means that you cannot sit on an opportunity and think it will always wait until you're ready to explore it. The minute you sleep on an opportunity, you will lose out. We made this mistake a few times as entrepreneurs. When you lose out on an opportunity or opportunities, you will be forced to let go of the things you cannot change—not just as an entrepreneur—but also for life in general.

As an entrepreneur, I recall when we had the opportunity to add another business to our portfolio. This was a huge deal. We would have been tapping into an area, not only of convenience, but unlimited possibility and not to mention that it would've added at the minimum another one hundred thousand dollars to our bank account in less than a year.

Wife. Mom. Entrepreneur.

Due to so many things that we did wrong, we completely let this opportunity slip through our fingers. As you can imagine, we were devastated. We dwelled on this unfortunate situation for a few days. We did learn our lesson and chalked it up to being something that was now out of our hands. We could not change what we missed, but we could learn from it as well as teach others. Let your business stress be your business success. We will stand on one thousand no's to get one yes.

We apply this type of thinking to all aspects of our life as *Wife. Mom. Entrepreneur.* When it's out of your hands, quickly move on. Police your thoughts. The cops have a saying to the dwellers at a crime scene, "There's nothing more to see around here people. Move on." Sweep your mind with that thought.

It's Out of Your Hands

- ✓ **NOTE**: Success for most of us does not come overnight. It's countless days and nights, reinventing yourself and changing your ideas to do what works best for you, your company, or the brand you're creating.
- ✓ Do not ever let failure deter you from your goals. Failure and some bad decisions come with the territory of business.
- ✓ Your business will become stagnate when you dwell. Quickly move on.
- ✓ There is much importance in seeing things through. By seeing things through, you can limit missed opportunities.
- ✓ Bounce back and know that there are other deals and business opportunities that will fit your business.
- ✓ Take all bad business deals, wrong negotiations, and failures as a learning curve.

NOTES

Collaborate/Partner

A collaboration/partnership is an agreement to accomplish a mutual goal by two or more persons or companies or between a person and a company. They share resources, human capital, gains, losses, and knowledge of the business' mission.

Thank God for blessing me with a sister friend with a like-mind! Although having each other was and still is a blessing, we recognized early on through trial and error, that the need for a team was important for the survival of our business. We identified our reason for failure was because we lacked collaborations, partnerships, and company teamwork. We vowed to never put ourselves or our business in a predicament to lose or fail. You can find a support team in the form of a collaboration or partnership with individuals or other businesses. If you are already in business and have employees, you can develop a team according to their skill sets and use them for a specific goal. If you do not have employees as of yet, don't worry. We will discuss how you can build a team without having employees.

Check out a few of our How To's:

Collaborating/Partnerships

- ✓ Think about why you need to collaborate/partner with another business/individual.
- ✓ Identify which business credentials and/or skills are essential for getting the job done successfully.
- ✓ Collaborate/partner with only trustworthy and reliable persons and companies.
- ✓ Be sure that you and your company mutually benefits from the agreement.
- ✓ Make sure to put everything in writing. Be descriptive of the responsibilities of all parties involved.
- ✓ Respect the collaboration/partnership for its differences and uniqueness. Each side brings something to the table. It does not matter who is doing more as long as the agreement is being respected and executed in a fashion that leads to success. It's all about attaining the goal. Keep in mind the reason for the collaboration/partnership.

Team-up Employees

- ✓ Choose the employees who are ready to prove themselves—the ones who are already motivated and

- demonstrate their leadership skills and interest in the company's mission.
- ✓ Make sure everyone is aware of the mission and vision for the business.
- ✓ Launch the purpose and make sure that all persons are aware of their purpose and function in getting the job done.
- ✓ Everyone must be made aware that they are a team, not in a group. For example, teams are required to lean on each other because of their diverse knowledge and skills, so respect must be present at all times. A group of people may all have the same skills and knowledge and aim to complete the same task.

Building A Team

- ✓ Register with a volunteer organization.
- ✓ Post ads on Craig's List.
- ✓ Contact your local universities for interns.
- ✓ Market your need for volunteers/interns on social media.

Always Remember:
Too often we have seen entrepreneurs lose sight of the mission because of greed. They try to keep all the money for themselves, not wanting to pay people for their services or expertise, or become unwilling to partner up or collaborate because of the fear to share the money and success.

Wife. Mom. Entrepreneur.

Remember, it's not all about the money. It's about the image of the business and successfully achieving company goals and duties. The money will come. Let it be about the outcome of consistently getting the job done right. Share the success when it's needed. You may gain a trustworthy, business partnership that brings a lot of wealth and a trusting image to your brand. More importantly, let your company's work speak for itself and the clients and customers will be willing to pay for whatever your company has to offer.

    We have created a checklist to use when you are teaming up:

Collaborate/Partner

Company/Individual	Reason for the collaboration	Credentials/Skills

> "The more you praise and celebrate your life, the more there is in life to celebrate."
>
> OPRAH WINFREY

Celebrating Small and Large Achievements

It's a big deal. It's a celebration! If there's one thing I love to do, it's to celebrate. As stated earlier in the book, we told you about our birthdays. We love to celebrate everything. I don't care if it's because the supermarket had everything in stock that was on my list; I caught my train on-time; I made it to the post office; or I got my hair done and prepared dinner all before my favorite show *Modern Family* came on—I'm celebrating!

Ladies, we need to learn to celebrate big and small achievements in our lives. The feeling of achievement is so comforting and it boosts your will to keep achieving. When we stop to celebrate small goals, it builds confidence, makes us set bigger goals, and more importantly, it's actual proof of what we set out to do and accomplish.

Wife. Mom. Entrepreneur.

Check out 8 simple ways to celebrate your accomplishments:

1. Pour yourself a glass of wine.
2. Write down your success in a journal.
3. Pat yourself on the back.
4. Tell the world! Go to your social media page and share your success. (This can encourage others too.)
5. Buy something. Don't go overboard unless it was a BIG accomplishment.
6. Take a spa day.
7. Take the day off.
8. Check that item off of your "To-Do" list.

Celebrating Small and Large Achievements

T I P S

Always Remember:

Make a list of your accomplishments and celebrate.

1. What is my smallest achievement this year?

2. What is my largest achievement this year?

3. How will I celebrate those achievements?

> "Sing so loud that the music drowns out the sounds of the naysayers. One day they'll be singing your song."
>
> JATAWNY MUCKELVENE CHATMON

God Bless My Naysayers

"Are you crazy? You are going to give up all of your benefits? What if your business fails?"

This is the most important time to show up and show out! If for no other reason, let this be the reason you finally get behind the wheel and drive. Let your naysayers be your motivation to get your job done. When I was leaving my career at one of New York's prestigious universities, I had so many people telling me it wasn't a good idea. I had people asking me about the fear of no longer earning a pension. When Lanise decided to leave her career, she had just returned from an all-expense paid training in London.

We had great jobs, but were not fulfilled. Lanise's husband was just as supportive of her decision to seek after her dreams as my husband. We knew once we had our husband's support that no one else's thoughts of our decision mattered.

Naysayers are everywhere. Your biggest naysayers will usually be your close family and friends. Don't be upset. They can't understand what God has put in your heart and

Wife. Mom. Entrepreneur.

they cannot understand or even know how you can have such drive and ambition to create your own life. The Bible is filled with naysayers. In Exodus, God famines Israel. He provided them with desert land because of their lack of faith in his promise to overflow the land with milk and honey (This is a great Bible story. Be sure to read it☺.)

You know you do not want to live a desert life. We chose faith over famine and we are enjoying our milk and honey. Thanks be to God. Let people doubt you and your works. Some will even hate on you or be envious because of your faith and courage. You know what has been placed in you, so have faith to carry out the mission to live a great life as a *Wife. Mom. Entrepreneur.*

> "So let's not get tired of doing what is good. At just the right time we will reap a harvest of blessings if we don't give up."
>
> GALATIANS 6:9 (NLT)

NOTES

Be Encouraged

Positive Affirmations to Live By

Be encouraged. It gets hard sometimes. Your strength will be tested and your weakness exposed. The wrong people in your ear can cause more harm than good. People will doubt you and attempt to deter you, so having a support system is very crucial.

You are the author of your story, so give birth to the gift God has placed in you. When you focus on what you truly want, you will find that leisure time lessens while goals start manifesting.

Be encouraged. We cannot tell you how many mistakes we've made, or how many times we did not learn the lesson that was in front of us, making an even bigger mess. You must be open to learn from your mistakes. Dust yourself off and start again. It can become weary, but the goal is to push on. The amount of times we've been frustrated and wanted to give up, cut our losses, and go get a job is endless.

Wife. Mom. Entrepreneur.

As a *Wife. Mom. Entrepreneur.,* listen to other successful people in all areas of life. You can learn so much from other women who have experienced what you are currently facing or may even have similar stories. Form a sisterhood where you are being positively encouraged as well as encouraging others. Do not entertain people who are not doing what you're trying to do. Having inspirational quotes, sayings, and affirmations posted in and around your home can be great motivation. Focus on what will keep you going! Prayer is everything! We encourage you to do whatever will help you keep a positive mindset.

Closing Notes

We hope that this book has been helpful for you. Its intention is to teach, encourage, and inspire. This book is the start of us sharing our triumphs, hang ups, and resources with all the women in the world. We intend to continue connecting with the wives, moms, and entrepreneurs all over the world.

We encourage you to visit us at
www.wifemomentrepreneur.com
and follow us:
Instagram: @WifeMomEntrepreneur
Periscope: WifeMomEntrepreneur
Twitter: @WifeMomEntrepreneur

Wife. Mom. Entrepreneur.

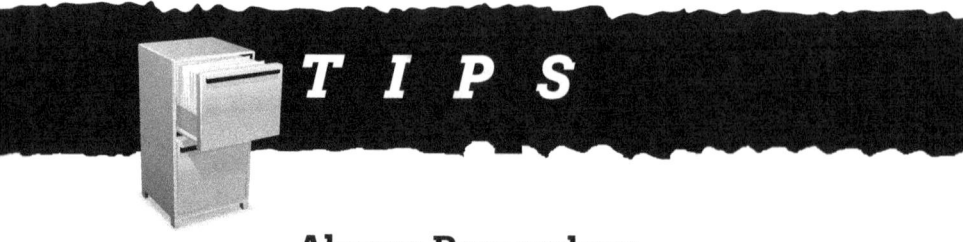

Always Remember:

You are strong. You are a woman and through Christ all things are possible. We are not perfect and can't balance all of our duties at all times. So, learn to juggle! You are an amazing *Wife. Mom. Entrepreneur.*

About the Authors

Lanise Herman-Thomas and Janine Smalls-Gueye have been wives for over seven years, moms for twenty-three years, and entrepreneurs for thirteen years. They are co-founders of a not-for-profit organization that specializes in development programs for the youth and young adults, and co-owners of a nutritional online boutique, clothing boutique, real estate investment company, and branding and management company for women who are wives, moms, and entrepreneurs. They both reside in New York City.

Herman-Thomas has been recognized and honored with an Image Entertainment Distinction Award for her many humanitarian efforts. She is also the Ambassador for *Surprise the Struggling,* an initiative that surprises at-risk teen girls and women with donated purses filled with hygienic toiletries.

Smalls-Gueye has written awarded grants totaling over $1 million.

NOTES

www.ingramcontent.com/pod-product-compliance
Lightning Source LLC
Chambersburg PA
CBHW052026290426
44112CB00014B/2396